W9-DDE-434

For Jason Reinstein,

Read and Enjoy!

Wendy Pfeffer

2004

Living on the Edge

High Mountains

WENDY PFEFFER

BENCHMARK BOOKS

MARSHALL CAVENDISH
NEW YORK

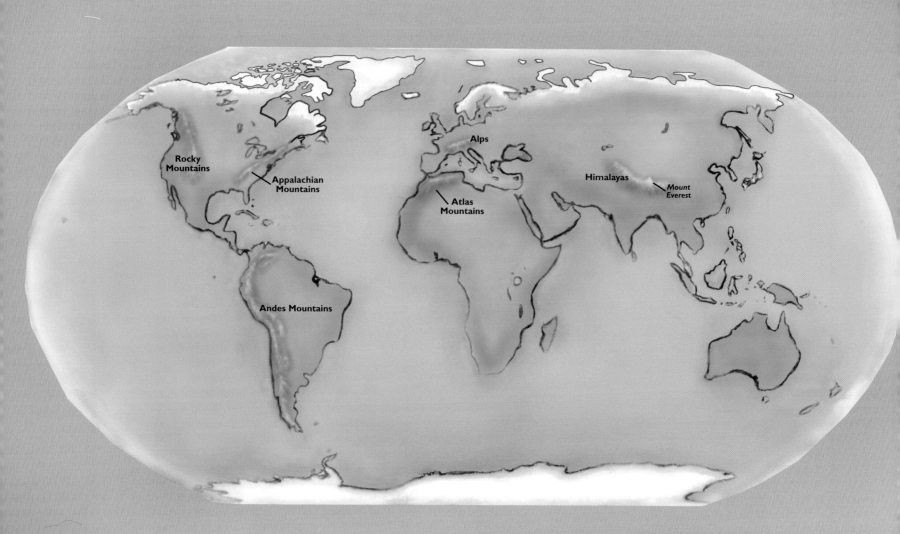

Rocky
Mountains

Appalachian
Mountains

Alps

Himalayas

Mount
Everest

Atlas
Mountains

Andes Mountains

Mountains of the World

Contents

The steep, rugged slopes of the Andes Mountains

Land Near the Sky

The higher one travels up a mountain, the colder and windier the air becomes. Steep, rugged slopes have low-growing vegetation and few places to find shelter. Strong winds sweep the soil away, leaving bare bedrock. Snow covers many mountains all year. Other mountains are carpeted with flowers in spring. Still others are strewn with jagged rocks. Mountains are as varied as the animals that make their homes there.

Pikas (PEA-kuhs or PIE-kuhs) live where plants grow. These tiny, tail-less animals work all day, collecting grass to make hay. Other mountain animals withstand frigid, blustery weather near the top, where plants are scarce. The world's highest habitat, at 22,000 feet (6,700 meters), is home to jumping spiders and small

5

A surefooted mountain goat surveys the world below.

insects called springtails. Jumping spiders hide under stones or plants. They are sharp-eyed hunters that can leap forty times their body length to grab prey. A spring-tail is a tiny, wingless insect with a forked tail under its abdomen that lets it spring several inches into the air. Springtails feed on fungi, bacteria, and decaying plants.

A jumping spider, one of the hardy animals that is able to survive on Earth's highest peaks

Hardy, surefooted animals tread the rugged terrain above the timberline. Yaks haul heavy loads in the Himalayas, the world's highest mountains. In the mountains of North America, bighorn sheep move with ease on craggy slopes and slippery rocks. Mountain goats spring across wide, deep crevices without hesitation.

Up high the mountain air is thin. At 18,000 feet (6,000 meters) there is little oxygen, only half the amount found at sea level. Animals need oxygen to breathe. Llamas, like all animals that live high in the mountains, have

A llama in the mountains of Peru

adapted by forming extra red blood cells. This increases the amount of oxygen their blood can carry.

Some animals cope with the harsh weather by hibernating, spending the winter in a kind of sleep. Others survive by migrating. They move up or down the mountains as the seasons change. Still others stay and face the cold, often with a warm coat of fur. One way or another all mountain animals have adaptations that help them stay alive in their habitat.

A Rocky Mountain bighorn sheep

Rocky Mountain Bighorns

Rocky Mountain bighorns live among the steep slopes, barren rock, frozen meadows, and jagged peaks of the Rocky Mountains. They get their name from their huge horns. Males grow long, curled horns. Females' horns are shorter. Bighorns are among the largest sheep in the world. Some weigh more than 330 pounds (150 kilograms), as much as a hefty football player, and can make breathtaking leaps

from one rocky ledge to another. A band of bighorns was once seen jumping off a 150-foot (46-meter) cliff—that's as high as Niagara Falls—and landing without harm.

Round hollows under their hooves grip the bare boulders and slippery rocks. Hard edges and rough pads let these surefooted mountaineers hold onto small cracks as they traverse cliffs that are almost straight up and down. To escape coyotes, cougars, and wolves, these skilled jumpers bound across crags and crevices too wide for predators to jump over. Not only are these sheep agile, they have good vision and can easily see animals coming.

Bighorns travel in groups of all females or all males up steep cliffs and over rugged crags, working their way above the timberline. They adapt to frigid winters by finding south-facing, sun-warmed slopes. Cold, blustery winds don't seem to bother these hardy creatures as long as the temperature stays above −4 degrees Fahrenheit (−20 degrees C). A fur coat and a thick layer of fat insulate them from freezing weather. In the spring they shed their heavy coats by rubbing against rocks and trees to help loosen the fur. Bighorn sheep appear

calm when they face an avalanche of falling rocks or snow. They look up, see the rocks or snow rolling toward them, move out of the way, and continue grazing. They feed on low-growing plants such as grasses, herbs, and sedges. Since these plants have little food value, sheep must eat a lot of them to survive.

A sheep's teeth grind food while its tongue mashes it. Its stomach has four chambers. Chewed food goes into the first chamber, where it is crushed. Muscles push those bits back up into the mouth. The sheep slowly chews the food again before it goes to the other three sections of the stomach to be digested. This second chewing is called cud chewing.

Cows, goats, and antelopes also chew their cud. After the first snowfall

These female bighorn sheep are shedding their winter coats.

bighorns chew the seed heads of plants and don't bother with the stems. This practice gives them the most nutrition and saves their energy for the coldest weather.

In fall males look for females. To attract them, males show off their large horns and chase away males with smaller horns. Some horns weigh 30 pounds (14 kilograms) and spread about 25 inches (64 centimeters). Bighorns don't shed their horns each year as deer and moose do. Their horns keep growing to make long-lasting weapons and shields. Thick hair protects their faces and two layers of bone shelter their brains from injury during clashes.

Before the mating season male bighorns fight to see who will be in charge. But during the harshest part of the winter, when snow piles up, they cooperate. They work together, pushing snow away with their muzzles. In deep snow they dig with their front legs, facing uphill so gravity helps each downward stroke uncover grasses to eat. Their survival depends on it. Sometimes, warm, moist winds help the sheep by thawing the snow and exposing grasses for them.

A bighorn sheep grazes on shoots poking through the snow.

In spring lambs are born, usually on a ledge. The overhanging rock shields them from predators. The mother nurses and protects her young. Eagles try to swoop

Bighorn males using their horns as weapons

A Rocky Mountain bighorn with a newborn lamb

down and carry the lambs away. Wolves may dash in and take them, too. A mother attacks predators with her horns to scare them off. Or she shoves her baby under her own body to hide it.

About a week after birth the lambs still nurse but follow their mother to find food. They learn survival skills early, playing "king of the mountain." One lamb tries to stay on top of a cliff while another tries to shove it off.

Bighorn lambs playing on a slope in June

A pika watches for predators from its talus.

Pikas

Pikas, the size and shape of guinea pigs, live at the timberline in Asia, Europe, and North America. Some scurry on meadowlike fields of broken rocks at 8,000 feet (2,440 meters) in the Rocky Mountains. Others graze on the slopes of Mount Everest in the Himalayan Mountains at 17,500 feet (5,337 meters) on rock-strewn terrain.

A pile of jumbled and tumbled rocks is called a talus (TAY-lus). To most pikas, a talus is home. It gives them shelter from freezing winds, a place to store food, and protection from predators. A pika must choose a talus with the proper-sized rocks. If the rocks are too large, predators can squeeze in. If the rocks are too small, the pika won't be able to move through its tunnels or have room to store its hay.

A pika collects grass for the winter.

A pika stays busy, either grazing when it is hungry or making hay to eat later. It grazes on grasses near the talus. A group of pikas can mow down a meadow. To make hay, a pika dashes back and forth from the talus to the meadow, which

may be a hundred feet away. It collects plant stalks and leaves by turning its head from one side to the other and biting off stems with its chisel-like teeth. Then the pika grips the plants between its teeth and carries as many as possible back to its talus. Sometimes when a pika scampers with long plants between its jaws, the plants get wedged between rocks, jolting the pika to a sudden stop.

Finally, the pika stacks the plants to dry and stores them for the winter. A hay pile may be 2 feet tall (0.5 meters) and almost 3 feet wide (1 meter) at the base. Pikas heap shrub branches on top to prevent the wind from scattering the hay around.

In spring pikas eat the flowers of columbine plants but ignore the stems because they are coated with a protective poison. When summer comes, the plants store the poison in their roots. So pikas wait for summer to chomp on the poison-free stems.

It may seem strange that pikas gather plants poisonous to them. But columbines prevent bacteria from invading hay piles and making them rot.

large polar bears together. Their black-brown hair sometimes drags on the ground. Even with their stout front legs, yaks are agile. They walk down icy mountains and dash across steep mountainsides. Courageous wild yaks defend themselves furiously. They will explode into a heated attack if provoked by humans, making them dangerous to hunt.

The wild yaks' smaller cousins are the hardworking, mild-mannered domestic yaks. Broad muzzles, rough tongues, and flexible lips let both wild and domestic yaks graze close to the ground on moss and lichens. They get water by eating snow. Yaks can survive frigid winters with temperatures of –40 degrees Fahrenheit (–40°C). Their shaggy coats, with soft undercoats over a layer of fat, prevent heat loss. Yaks spend summers on the snowfields at 20,000 feet (6,000 meters). During blizzards, which can occur even in early summer, they face away from the wind. This is unusual since most animals face into the wind.

High mountain animals must adapt to less oxygen in the air. Yaks, like llamas, have three times as many red blood cells as cattle living at lower elevations, which increases the amount of oxygen the blood can carry. Yaks also have large rib cages, huge lungs, and muscles that let them breathe deeply while traveling. As they inhale and exhale, they sound like locomotives chugging along.

Hardy domestic yaks have served Himalayan mountain people for more than four thousand years. On strong, sturdy legs they haul barley to be traded for salt and then carry the salt across the world's highest mountain range to trade for

"Mountain machines" carrying heavy loads in the thin air of Mount Everest

grain. They are surefooted on narrow trails, rocks, and glaciers. They wade through fast-flowing streams, and move belly-deep through snowdrifts. These "mountain machines" are so important in the Himalayas that the value of a man's worth is measured by the size of his herd.

Incredible Mountain Dwellers

Mountains and mountain animals come in different shapes and sizes. Many animals have developed special adaptations to fit the challenges of their mountain habitat.

Frigid weather, little oxygen, scarce food, barren rocks, strong winds, steep slopes, rugged terrain, and poisonous plants test even the hardiest creatures. Somehow these incredible mountain dwellers adapt to conditions that we would call hard and inhospitable but that they call home.

Other Animals Adapt and Survive

Wall Creepers, little birds that nest in crevices on cliffs and raise their young there, live 5,000 feet (1,800 meters) high in the Alps. In autumn they leave and move to lower levels. They survive by plucking insects and spiders out of cracks in the rocks.

A wall creeper on a rock ledge

A chamois leaps playfully in the snow.

Chamoises (SHAM-ee), goatlike antelopes of Eurasia, have shock-absorbing legs. To reach an upper ledge, they can leap 13 feet (4 meters) in the air. That's higher than a regulation basketball hoop.

Snow Leopards' tails are almost as long as the rest of their bodies. Animals that live where it is cold usually have small ears, tails, and feet to reduce heat loss. But this nocturnal prowler needs a long tail for balance when leaping over snowbanks and climbing up the steep slopes of Central Asia.

A snow leopard of Central Asia

Mountain Fish are specially adapted to swift-flowing mountain streams. Suckermouth catfish in the Andes have mouths that allow them to grip the stream bottom and not be dragged along with the current. Catfish don't have scales, so the water flows by with little drag. Strong tail muscles also help to control speed.

A spotted suckermouth catfish

Baby wolf spiders emerging from their egg case

Wolf Spiders survive on Mount Everest by eating small insects that are swept up on air currents. The female spider spins a cocoon around her eggs and carries it with her. If it rains she makes a shelter for it. When the sun comes out, she holds the sac up to dry. After the spiderlings hatch, she carries them on her back. But if one falls off, it is on its own.

Klipspringers, small antelopes, can leap 30 feet (9 meters), as long as a school bus, over deep crevices onto narrow ledges. They can land with all four feet together on a spot no larger than a cookie.

A male klipspringer on the lookout

ABOUT THE AUTHOR

Wendy Pfeffer, an award-winning author of fiction and nonfiction books, enjoyed an early career as a first grade teacher. Now a full-time writer, she visits schools, where she makes presentations and conducts writing workshops. She lives in Pennington, New Jersey, with her husband, Tom.

For Laurie Halse Anderson, Pat Brisson, Deborah Heiligman, Martha Hewson, Sally Keehn, Susan Korman, Joyce McDonald, Kay Winters, Elvira Woodruff, and Liz Bennett Bailey, the Authors of Bucks County, who share not only their expertise but their friendship. Thank you, all.

Thanks also to Jackie Ziegler, who read this manuscript, and to Kate Nunn, my fine editor.

Benchmark Books
Marshall Cavendish
99 White Plains Road
Tarrytown, New York 10591-9001

www.marshallcavendish.com

Text copyright © 2003 Wendy Pfeffer
Map by Sonia Chaghatzbanian
Map copyright © 2003 Marshall Cavendish Corporation

Library of Congress Cataloging-in-Publication Data

Pfeffer, Wendy, 1929-
High mountains / by Wendy Pfeffer.
p. cm. -- (Living on the edge)
Summary: Looks at the various kinds of animals, including mountain
goats, pikas, yaks, and bighorn sheep, that survive in the world's
tallest mountain ecosystems.
Includes bibliographical references and index.
ISBN 0-7614-1441-X
1. Mountain animals--Juvenile literature. [1. Mountain animals.] I.
Title. II. Living on the edge (New York, N.Y.)
QL113 .P44 2002
599.1753--dc21
2002003521

Photo Research by Candlepants, Inc.

Cover Photo: *Photo Researchers* Stephen J. Krasemann

The photographs in this book are used by permission and through the courtesy of: *Photo Researchers*: Art Wolf, 1, 29, 32;
Francois Gohier, 4–5, 8; Mark Newman, 10; Ken M. Johns, 14; Renee Lynn, 16; Tom and Pat Leeson, 15, 21; George D.
Lepp, 19, 20; Tom McHugh, 23; Alison Wright, 26; Mark Smith, 33; Nature's Images, Inc., 34; Craig K. Lorenz, back
cover. *Corbis*: W. Wayne Lockwood, M.D., 6; W. Perry Conway, 12–13, 15; George D. Lepp, 18; Kit Kittle, 24. *Animals
Animals*: Joe McDonald, 7; Lynn Stone, 11; Peter Baumann, 30; Robert Maier, 31; Ingrid Van Den Berg, 35.

Printed in Hong Kong

1 3 5 6 4 2